CW00530123

For Your Baby's
Dedication

Selected by

Peter Dainty

**kevin
mayhew**

What a miracle of creation
    a new baby is –
    almost unbelievable
    in its miniature perfection
    of fingers and toes,
    eyes, ears and nose.
Yet it is not just
    the amazing product
    of chemicals and genes,
    but the fruit of God's creative Spirit,
    a living person
    sent to teach us how to love.
For he was conceived in love,
    and now cries out
    instinctively
    to be loved.
And that is why,
    instinctively,
    we hold him in our arms
    and start to learn
    Love's lesson.

Peter Dainty

The Parents' Prayer

Heavenly Father,
   we thank you from our hearts
   for our new baby,
   whom you have sent into our lives
   and put into our care,
   so fragile, so helpless,
   so amazing, so appealing.
We welcome her with gentle love,
   and ask for grace and wisdom
   as we take on the responsibility
   for this new life,
   feeding, protecting, nursing,
   teaching and encouraging her

May she grow
   in strength and health,
   in knowledge and understanding,
   in eagerness and determination,
   in love and laughter,
   until she comes to know you
   as her Maker and Friend.
Then may she learn the joy
   of walking in your ways,
   through Jesus Christ our Lord.
Amen.

Peter Dainty

A Mother's Prayer

Loving Father,
   as I hold my baby
   in my arms
   and watch
   his every movement
   with loving delight,
   I am filled with a sense
   of gratitude and awe
   at such a precious gift.
Help me to care for him
   with gentleness
   and patience,
   knowing how much
   he depends on me,
   and how much
   he will learn
   from the way I treat him.

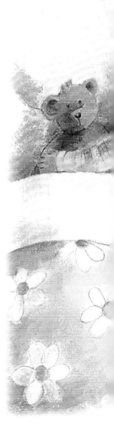

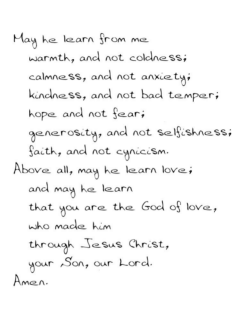

May he learn from me
  warmth, and not coldness;
  calmness, and not anxiety;
  kindness, and not bad temper;
  hope and not fear;
  generosity, and not selfishness;
  faith, and not cynicism.
Above all, may he learn love;
  and may he learn
  that you are the God of love,
  who made him
  through Jesus Christ,
  your Son, our Lord.
Amen.

Peter Dainty

The Pain and the Joy

Lord Jesus,
  I never thought,
  that pain and joy
  could be so closely bound,
  until I experienced it,
  in giving birth.
Help me to learn it also
  in the demanding
  daily routine
  of nappy-changing,
  feeding, bathing
  and trying to get my baby
  to sleep (and keep myself
  awake).
Sometimes, when I'm tired,
  I feel that there is nothing else
  in all the world
  but my baby and me,

and nothing else out there
  beyond these four walls
  except the clinic.
But when my baby smiles,
  or gurgles,
  or reaches out her hand
  to clutch my nose,
  or just lies there,
  sleeping peacefully,
  I know it's all worth while.
It won't always be like this;
  she will grow up all too soon
  and I will probably wish
  she was a baby again.
So help me, Lord,
  not only to survive
  the exhausting demands
  of these first weeks
  but to appreciate
  their delights as well –
  while they're still here.

Peter Dainty

A Father's Prayer

Thank you, heavenly Father,
  for my baby son.
May I be a good father to him
May I be always there
  to protect him.
May I be able to help him
  to learn and to grow,
  in body and in spirit.
Help me to show him the difference
  between right and wrong,
  and encourage him
  to choose the right
  by being a good example to him

May I help him
   to discover his strengths
   and develop his gifts;
   show him how to make
   his own choices
   and to learn from his mistakes.
May I be quick to praise his success
   and to stand by him in failure.
May I be there to support him
   through adversity
   and lead him to trust in you
   in all circumstances.
Then may he know
   that even if I should let him down,
   he has a Father in heaven
   who never will.
Amen.

Peter Dainty

A Grandparent's Prayer

It doesn't seem five minutes, Lord,
  since I held my own baby daughter
  in my arms.
Now she has her own daughter
  a new generation.
Thank you, Lord,
  for this wonderful gift.
I'd forgotten how small and light
  new babies are.
It's lovely to hold one again,
  especially another
  member of the family.
What fun it will be
  to have her around,
  and see her growing up.

Help me not to be
    too possessive or interfering,
    but please give me
    the health and strength
    to be ready to help out
    when needed.

I'm so looking forward
    to those visits to the park,
    trips to the seaside,
    family games, watching TV,
    bedtime prayers, going to church,
    school plays, pantomimes. . .

But there I go, Lord,
    I'm planning her life already.
Please give me the grace to leave
    something for you to do.
Amen.

Peter Dainty

13

An Elder Sister or Brother

Hello there, new baby!
Let's get a few things straight.
You need to know that
   you are the best baby in the world.
Until you came along,
   I was the baby in this family.
I've done the job long enough;
   now it's your turn.
You can't do very much yet,
   but you do it very well.
In fact, that's what you're best at,
   that's what everyone expects of you.

As the months go on,
   it'll get more interesting,
   and don't worry,
   I'll be there to help;
   just watch me.
Me? What am I going to do?
Well, thanks to you,
   I've been promoted.
You may be
   the world's best baby,
   but I've just become
   the world's best toddler!

F Mary Callan

An Adopted Child

Lord, you know how difficult it was
   for us to accept
   that we would never
   have a child.
Our whole world collapsed,
   our life seemed empty.

Thank you for redirecting
   our longing
   into genuine love
   for this child
   that we are to adopt.

Give us the wisdom and strength
   to make this child
   feel 'at home' with us,
   and know that he has been given to us
   as a special gift from you.

Lord, we know it won't be easy.
This child of ours will have times
   of uncertainty and insecurity.
He will want to know
   who his natural mother was
   and why she gave him up.
He may feel vulnerable
   with other children.

Give to us, Lord,
   who have been adopted
   into your family through Christ,
   the gift of reassurance
   in the love we feel
   for each other
   so that he may never doubt
   the priceless gift he represents.
Amen.

John Rayne-Davis

A Baby Born with Special Needs

All children are special to you, Lord.
But this child is very special indeed,
   deserving of extra love and support.
Please, Lord, allow him to reach
   his full potential as a person.

I know, Lord, that life will not be easy;
   frustration, anger, isolation
   will threaten him constantly.
He will always stand out in a crowd
   and may suffer ridicule and humiliation.

Lord, teach us to discern
   the talents, the gifts, the abilities
   you have given him,
   and to learn from them,
   so that our lives are enriched by his.

May he always feel appreciated
   and cherished, because
   there are many around him
   who love him
   and want the best for him.
Amen.

John Rayne-Davis

The Parents of a Special Needs Baby

Why us, God?

Why our baby?

How can you condemn
    a helpless child to such a fate?

How we envy other parents
    and their babies!

Help us, Lord!
Our anger is helping
    neither us nor our baby.

Help us to discover and value
   the positive things
   which make our baby unique –
   a person like no other.

Lord, you have made her
   in your image and likeness.
Help us to care for her
   in such a way
   that she is happy and fulfilled.
Grant us all the strength we need
   to move forward as a family
   in hope and love.
Amen.

John Rayne-Davis

Prayer for a Sick Child

Lord, hear our anxious prayer
    for . . .(name). . . who is in such pain
    and discomfort.
We weep to see him
    struggling like this,
    so weak and helpless.

We long to see him
full of health and vigour (again).
May his crying give way
to a healing sleep
so that he awakes to life.
We entrust him, Lord,
to your caring love.

Peter Dainty

Prayer for a Stillborn Child

Heavenly Father,
  we cannot understand
  the meaning of this life
  that was never to be lived.
We cry out to you
  in our anguish, loss and pain,
  and think for a while
  of what might have been.
We ask you to understand
  our frustration and our anger.
Maybe we shall be able
  to make sense of it all
  one day.

But, for now,
   we can only hold him
   in our helpless arms
   and marvel at the mystery of life,
   even in death.
Then we must hand him back to you
   to give him a better life
   elsewhere;
   for we cannot give him life here.
Father, have mercy on him
   and on us,
   for the sake of your Son,
   Jesus Christ.
Amen.

Peter Dainty

Heavenly Father,
   bless our children
   with healthful bodies,
   with good understandings,
   with the graces and gifts
   of your Holy Spirit,
   with sweet dispositions
   and holy habits;
   and sanctify them throughout,
   in their bodies, souls and spirits,
   and keep them blameless
   to the coming
   of our Lord Jesus Christ.
Amen.

Jeremy Taylor (1613-67)

Almighty God
   and heavenly Father,
   we thank you for the children
   which you have given us.
Give us also wisdom to train them
   in your faith, fear and love,
   that as they advance in years,
   they may grow in grace,
   through Jesus Christ our Lord.
Amen.

John Cosin (1595-1672)

I pray for you a joyous life,
  honour, estate and good repute;
  no sigh from your heart,
  no tear from your eye,
  no hindrance on your path,
  no shadow on your face,
  until you lie down
  in that mansion
  in the arms of Christ benign.

A Celtic blessing

The blessing of the Holy Three,
little love, be the gift to thee:
wisdom,
peace
and purity.

A Celtic prayer which a mother
whispers into the ear of her baby.

Gentle Jesus, meek and mild,
look upon this little child.
Pity her simplicity,
suffer her to come to thee.
Let her, above all, fulfil
God her heavenly Father's will,
never his good Spirit grieve,
only to his glory live.

Charles Wesley (1707-88)
adapted

God, make this child a shining light
   within the world to glow
   a little flame that burneth bright,
   wherever he may go.
God, make his life a joyful song
   that comforteth the sad,
   that helpeth others to be strong
   and makes the singer glad.
God, make his life a trusty staff,
   whereon the weak may rest,
   so that what health and strength he hath
   may serve his neighbours best.
God, make his life a constant hymn
   of wonder and of praise,
   of faith and hope that never dim
   and love in all his ways.

Matilda Barbara Bethan-Edwards (1836-1919)
adapted

First published in 2004 by

KEVIN MAYHEW LTD
Buxhall, Stowmarket, Suffolk, IP14 3BW
E-mail: info@kevinmayhewltd.com

9 8 7 6 5 4 3 2 1 0

ISBN 1 84417 348 8

Catalogue No. 1500760

Designed by Angela Selfe
Illustrations by Angela Palfrey

Printed and bound in China